Collins

SNAP
REVISION
FORCES &
ELECTRICITY

AQA GCSE Physics

AQA
GCSE
PHYSICS

REVISE TRICKY
TOPICS IN A SNAP

SNAP REVISION
FORCES & ELECTRICITY

Contents

Published by Collins
An imprint of HarperCollinsPublishers
1 London Bridge Street,
London, SE1 9GF

© HarperCollinsPublishers Limited 2016

9780008218133

First published 2016

10 9 8 7 6 5 4 3 2 1

British Library Cataloguing in Publication Data.

A CIP record of this book is available from the British Library.

Printed in United Kingdom by Martins the Printers

ACKNOWLEDGEMENTS

The author and publisher are grateful to the copyright holders for permission to use quoted materials and images.

Every effort has been made to trace copyright holders and obtain their permission for the use of copyright material. The author and publisher will gladly receive information enabling them to rectify any error or omission in subsequent editions. All facts are correct at time of going to press.

HT Higher Tier content

How To Use This Book

To get the most out of this revision guide, just work your way through the book in the order it is presented.

This is how it works:

Revise

Clear and concise revision notes help you get to grips with the topic

Revise

Key Points and Key Words explain the important information you need to know

Revise

A Quick Test at the end of every topic is a great way to check your understanding

Practise

Practice questions for each topic reinforce the revision content you have covered

Review

The Review section is a chance to revisit the topic to improve your recall in the exam

Forces – An Introduction

You must be able to:

- Describe the difference between a vector and a scalar quantity
- Use vectors to describe the forces involved when objects interact
- Calculate the resultant of two forces that act in a straight line
- Explain the difference between mass and weight
- Recognise and use the symbol for proportionality
- **HT** Use vector diagrams to show resolution and addition of forces.

Scalar and Vector Quantities

- A scalar quantity has magnitude (size) only, e.g. number of apples.
- A vector quantity has magnitude and direction, e.g. velocity, which shows the speed *and* the direction of travel.
- Arrows can be used to represent vector quantities:
  - the length of the arrow shows the magnitude
  - the arrow points in the direction that the vector quantity is acting.
- Forces are vector quantities.
- The diagram shows the forces acting on a boat. The arrows indicate the direction they are acting.

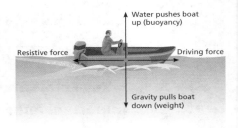

Water pushes boat up (buoyancy)

Resistive force

Driving force

Gravity pulls boat down (weight)

Contact and Non-Contact Forces

- A force occurs when two or more objects interact.
- Forces are either:
  - contact forces – the objects are actually touching, e.g. the tension as two people pull against one another
  - non-contact forces – the objects are not touching, e.g. the force of gravity acts even when the objects are not touching.

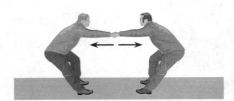

Contact Forces	Non-Contact Forces
Friction	Gravitational force
Air-resistance / drag	Electrostatic force
Tension	Magnetic force
Normal contact force	
Upthrust	

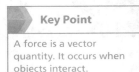

Key Point

A force is a vector quantity. It occurs when objects interact.

Gravity

- Gravity is a force of attraction between all masses.
- The force of gravity close to Earth is due to the gravitational field around the planet.
- The mass of an object is related to the amount of matter it contains and is constant.
- Weight is the force acting on an object due to gravity.
- The weight of an object depends on the gravitational field strength where the object is and is directly proportional to its mass.

- This symbol is used to indicate two things are proportional: ∝.

weight = mass × gravitational field strength

$W = mg$

Weight (W) is measured in newtons (N).
Mass (m) is measured in kilograms (kg).
Gravitational field strength (g) is measured in newtons per kilogram (N/kg).

Resultant Forces

- When more than one force acts on an object, these forces can be seen as a single force that has the same effect as all the forces acting together.
- This is called the resultant force.

HT Vector Diagrams

- A free body diagram can be used to show different forces acting on an object (see the diagram on the boat on page 4).
- Scale vector diagrams are used to illustrate the overall effect when more than one force acts on an object:
  - The forces are added together to find a single resultant force, including both magnitude and direction.
  - The vectors are added head to tail and a resultant force arrow is drawn.

$$F_R = F_1 + F_2$$

- Scale vector diagrams can also be used when a force is acting in a diagonal direction:
  - Expressing the diagonal force as two forces at right-angles to each other can help to work out what effect the force will have.
  - The force F_R can be broken down into F_1 and F_2.
  - F_1 is the same length as the length of F_R in the horizontal direction.
  - F_2 is the same length as the length of F_R in the vertical direction.
  - F_R is also the vector found by adding F_1 and F_2 head to tail.

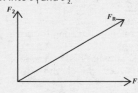

Key Point

The gravitational field strength (g) on Earth is 10N/kg, so a student with a mass of 50kg has a weight of (50 × 10 =) 500N.

10N
Frictional forces

15N
Pushing force

Resultant force ⟶ 5N

Key Point

Weight is a force that can be measured using a newtonmeter (a calibrated spring-balance). The unit of measurement is newtons (N).
weight ∝ mass

Key Words

scalar
vector
force
contact force
non-contact force
gravity
mass
weight
resultant
HT free body diagram

Quick Test

1. How is a scalar quantity different from a vector quantity?
2. Use an example to explain what is meant by 'non-contact force'.
3. An astronaut with a mass of 80kg stands on the moon. What is his weight? (g = 1.6N/kg)
4. A car travels in a straight line to the east with a driving force of 500N. If total frictional forces are 400N, what is the resultant force and in which direction does it act?

Forces in Action

You must be able to:

- Describe the energy transfers involved when work is done
- Explain why changing the shape of an object can only happen when more than one force is applied to the object
- Interpret data showing the relationship between force and extension
- Perform force calculations for balanced objects
- Explain how levers and gears work.

Work Done and Energy Transfer

- When a force causes an object to move, work is done on the object.
- This is because it requires energy to move the object.
- One joule of work is done when a force of one newton causes a displacement of one metre: 1 joule = 1 newton metre.

> work done = force × distance (moved along the line of action of the force)
>
> $W = Fs$ ◄

Work done (W) is measured in joules (J).
Force (F) is measured in newtons (N).
Distance (s) is measured in metres (m).

- When work is done, energy transfers take place within the system, e.g. work done to overcome friction causes an increase in heat energy.

Key Point

Overcoming forces requires energy. When a force is used to move an object, work is done on the object. The movement of the object is called displacement.

Forces and Elasticity

- To change the shape of an object, more than one force must be applied, e.g. a spring must be pulled from both ends to stretch it.
- If the object returns to its original shape after the forces are removed, it was elastically deformed.
- If the object does *not* return to its original shape, it has been inelastically deformed.
- The extension of an elastic object is directly proportional to the applied force, i.e. they have a linear relationship and produce a straight line on a force–extension graph.
- However, once the limit of proportionality has been exceeded:
  - doubling the force will no longer exactly double the extension
  - the relationship becomes non-linear
  - a force–extension graph will stop being a straight line.
- This equation applies to the linear section of a force–extension graph:

> force = spring constant × extension
>
> $F = ke$ ◄

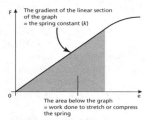

The gradient of the linear section of the graph = the spring constant (k)

The area below the graph = work done to stretch or compress the spring

Force (F) is measured in newtons (N).
Spring constant (k) is measured in newtons per metre (N/m).
Extension (e) is measured in metres (m).

- This also applies to the compression of an elastic object.
- The spring constant indicates how easy it is to stretch or compress a spring – the higher the spring constant, the stiffer the spring.
- A force that stretches or compresses a spring stores elastic potential energy in the spring.
- The amount of work done and the energy stored are equal, provided the spring does not go past the limit of proportionality.

Key Point

The work done to stretch or compress a spring is equal to the energy stored in the spring, provided the spring has not been inelastically deformed.

Investigate the relationship between force and extension of a spring.

Sample Method	Considerations, Mistakes and Errors
1. Set up the equipment as shown. 2. Add 100g (1N) to the mass holder. 3. Measure the extension of the spring and record the result. 4. Repeat steps 2 to 3 for a range of masses from 1N to 10N.	• The extension is the total increase in length from the original unloaded length. It is *not* the total length or the increase each time. • Adding too many masses can stretch the spring too far, which means repeat measurements cannot be made.

Variables	Hazards and Risks
• The independent variable is the one deliberately changed – in this case, the force on the spring. • The dependent variable is the one that is measured – the extension.	• The biggest hazard in this experiment is masses falling onto the experimenter's feet. To minimise this risk, keep masses to the minimum needed for a good range of results.

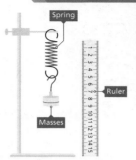

Moments, Levers and Gears

- When a force causes an object to rotate about a **pivot** point, the turning effect is called **moment** of a force.

$$\text{moment of a force} = \text{force} \times \text{distance}$$

$$M = Fd$$

> Moment of a force (M) is measured in newton metres (Nm).
> Force (F) is measured in newtons (N).
> Distance (d) is the perpendicular distance from the pivot to the line of action of the force in metres (m).

- If an object is balanced, the total clockwise moment about the pivot equals the total anticlockwise moment about that pivot:
$F_1 \times d_1 = F_2 \times d_2$

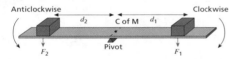

Perpendicular distance between the line of action of the force and the pivot

Line of force

A force of 500N is positioned 1m from the middle of a seesaw. It is balanced by another force 2m from the middle. How large is the second force?

$500 \times 1 = F_2 \times 2$ ← Substitute the given values into the equation $F_1 \times d_1 = F_2 \times d_2$.

$F_2 = \dfrac{500 \times 1}{2} = 250N$ ← Divide both sides by 2 to leave F_2 on its own.

- **Levers** and **gears** can be used to:
  - transmit the rotational effects of forces
  - magnify either the size of the applied force or the distance the force moves over.
- When the applied force moves further than the transmitted force, the force is increased.
- When the applied force is bigger than the transmitted force, the distance is increased.

> ### Key Point
> The range in an experiment needs to be large enough to show a pattern.

> ### Key Words
> work
> elastically deformed
> inelastically deformed
> extension
> limit of proportionality
> compression
> spring constant
> pivot
> moment
> lever
> gear

Quick Test

1. Calculate the work done when a force of 200N is used to move an object 50cm.
2. A plank is pivoted in the middle. A 30N force is placed 50cm from the pivot. How far from the pivot, on the other side, would a 40N force need to be applied to balance the plank?

Pressure and Pressure Differences

Forces

You must be able to:

- Recall and use the equation for pressure
- Describe a simple model of the Earth's atmosphere
- Explain why atmospheric pressure varies with height
- HT Explain the effect of fluid density on pressure
- HT Calculate difference in pressure at different depths in a liquid
- HT Explain the origin of upthrust.

Pressure in a Fluid

- A fluid can either be a liquid or a gas.
- As particles move around in a fluid, they collide with the surface of objects in the fluid or the surface of the container.
- The collisions create a force normal (at right-angles) to the surface.
- The link between pressure, force and area is described with the following equation:

LEARN

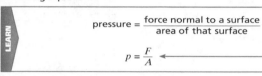

$$\text{pressure} = \frac{\text{force normal to a surface}}{\text{area of that surface}}$$

$$p = \frac{F}{A}$$

> **Key Point**
>
> Pressure is caused by particles colliding with a surface.

Pressure (p) is measured in pascals (Pa).
Force (F) is measured in newtons (N).
Area (A) is measured in metres squared (m²).

- If the pressure acts on a bigger area, it will produce a larger force.

$$\text{pressure} = \frac{\text{small force}}{\text{small area}}$$

$$\text{pressure} = \frac{\text{large force}}{\text{large area}}$$

Atmospheric Pressure

- The atmosphere is a relatively thin layer of air around the Earth.
- The greater the altitude, the less dense the atmosphere and the lower the atmospheric pressure.
- At a high altitude there is less air above a surface than at lower altitudes, so there is a smaller weight of air acting on the surface and the equation $p = \frac{F}{A}$ will result in a lower pressure.

Top of the atmosphere

1m² column of air

Mass = 10⁴kg

Increasing gravitational force = increasing pressure

Sea level

HT Pressure in a Column of Liquid

- Pressure at a particular point in a column of liquid depends on:
  - the height of the column above the point
  - the density of the liquid.
- The higher the column and the more dense the liquid:
  - the greater the weight above the point
  - the greater the force on the surface at that point
  - the greater the pressure.

> **Key Point**
>
> The particle model explaining pressure is a very good example of a model explaining a scientific idea.

- The pressure can be calculated with the equation below:

pressure = height of the column × density of the liquid × gravitational field strength

$p = h\rho g$

A diver descends from the surface to a depth of 25m.
The gravitational field strength is 10N/kg and the density of water is 1000kg/m³.

Work out the increase in pressure.

$p = h\rho g = 25 \times 1000 \times 10$
$p = 250\,000\text{Pa}$

Substitute the given values into the equation.

Don't forget the units.

Pressure (p) is measured in in pascals (Pa).
Height of column (h) is measured in metres (m).
Density (ρ) is measured in kilograms per metre cubed (kg/m³).

Upthrust

- When an object is submerged in a liquid, there is a greater height of liquid above the bottom surface than above the top surface.
- The bottom surface experiences a greater pressure than the top surface and this creates a resultant force upwards.
- The upwards force exerted by a fluid on a submerged object is called upthrust.
- An object floats when its weight is equal to the upthrust and sinks when its weight is greater than the upthrust.
- The density of an object indicates if it will float or sink.
- An object less dense than the liquid:
  - displaces a volume of liquid greater than its own weight so it will rise to the surface
  - will float with some of the object remaining below surface
  - displaces liquid of equal weight to the object.
- If an object has a low density, more of the object will remain above the surface.
- An object denser than the surrounding liquid cannot displace enough liquid to equal its own weight so it sinks.
- No matter how dense an object is, the size of the upthrust is equal to the weight of liquid displaced.

Key Point

The deeper an object is submerged, the greater the pressure.

A more dense liquid exerts a greater pressure.

The Density of an Object Affects if it will Float or Sink

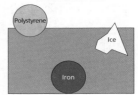

Quick Test

1. Describe how the particles in a fluid create pressure.
2. Atmospheric pressure is 100 000Pa. What force does this apply on an area of 0.1m²?
3. An object floats in water. 90% of the object is below the water line. The density of water is 1000kg/m³.
   Estimate the density of the object.
4. Find the pressure difference between a submarine at a depth of 100m and another submarine at a depth of 300m.
   density of water = 1000kg/m³,
   gravitational field strength = 10N/kg

Key Words

fluid
normal
pressure
atmosphere
altitude
dense
upthrust
displace

Forces and Motion

You must be able to:

- Describe displacement in terms of both magnitude and direction
- Recall typical values for common speeds
- Calculate speed from measurements of distance and time
- HT Give examples of objects with constant speed but changing velocity
- Explain the motion of objects using Newton's first law
- Draw and interpret distance–time graphs.

Distance and Displacement

- **Distance** is a scalar quantity:
  - It is how far an object moves.
  - It does not take into account the direction an object is travelling in or even if it ends up back where it started.
- **Displacement** is a vector quantity:
  - It has a magnitude, which describes how far the object has travelled from the origin, measured in a straight line.
  - It has a direction, which is the direction of the straight line.

Path of travel

Displacement

Speed

- The **speed** of an object is a measure of how fast it is travelling.
- It is a scalar quantity measured in metres per second (m/s).
- The speed that a person can walk, run or cycle depends on factors like age, fitness, terrain and distance.
- Some typical speeds can be seen below:

Method of Travel	Speed (m/s)	Method of Travel	Speed (m/s)
Walking	1.5	Motorway driving	30
Running	3	High speed trains	75
Cycling	6	Commercial aircraft	250
City driving	12	Speed of sound in air	330

- Most things (including sound) do not travel at a constant speed, so it is often the average speed over a period of time that is used.

distance travelled = speed × time

$$s = vt$$

Distance (s) is measured in metres (m).
Speed (v) is measured in metres per second (m/s).
Time (t) is measured in seconds (s).

Velocity

- **Velocity** is a vector quantity.
- It is the speed of an object in a given direction.
- HT When travelling in a straight line, an object with constant speed also has constant velocity.

Forces

HT If the object is *not* travelling in a straight line, e.g. it is turning a corner:
- the speed can still be constant
- the velocity will change, because the direction has changed.

HT An object moving in a circle:
- is constantly changing direction, so it is constantly changing velocity
- is accelerating even if it is travelling at constant speed.

HT Orbiting planets are an example of this – it is the force of gravity that causes the acceleration.

> ### HT ▶ Key Point
>
> An object travelling in a circle can have constant speed, but its velocity is still changing.

Newton's First Law

- Newton's first law is often stated as: an object will remain in the same state of motion unless acted on by an external force.
- When the resultant force acting on an object is zero:
  - if the object is stationary, it remains stationary
  - if the object is moving, it continues to move at the same speed and in the same direction, i.e. at constant velocity.

> HT This tendency for objects to continue in the same state of motion is called inertia.

- The velocity (speed or direction) of an object will only change if there is a resultant force acting on it.
- For a car travelling at a steady speed, the driving force is balanced by the resistive forces.

Distance–Time Graphs

- A distance–time graph can be used to represent the motion of an object travelling in a straight line.
- The speed of the object is found from the gradient (slope) of the line.
- The graph on the right shows:
  ❶ A stationary object.
  ❷ An object moving at a constant speed of 2m/s.
  ❸ An object moving at a greater constant speed of 3m/s.

HT If an object is accelerating, the distant–time graph will be a curve.

HT For an accelerating object, its speed at a particular time is found by:
- drawing a tangent to the curve at the point in time
- working out the gradient of the tangent.

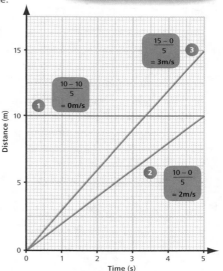

Constant Speed
Resistive force ←——————→ Driving force

❶ $\dfrac{10-10}{5} = 0\text{m/s}$

❸ $\dfrac{15-0}{5} = 3\text{m/s}$

❷ $\dfrac{10-0}{5} = 2\text{m/s}$

> ### Key Point
>
> A distance–time graph can be used to calculate speed.

> ### Key Words
>
> distance
> displacement
> speed
> velocity
> HT accelerating
> HT inertia

> ### Quick Test
>
> 1. Describe the difference between distance and displacement.
> 2. Work out the speed of a car that travels 1km in 50 seconds.
> 3. What does the gradient of a distance–time graph show?

Forces and Acceleration

You must be able to:

- Apply Newton's second law to situations where objects are accelerating
- Estimate the magnitude of everyday accelerations
- Draw and interpret velocity–time graphs.

Acceleration

- The **acceleration** of an object is a measure of how quickly it speeds up, slows down or changes direction.

$$\text{acceleration} = \frac{\text{change in velocity}}{\text{time taken}}$$

$$a = \frac{\Delta v}{t}$$

- When an object slows down, the change in velocity is negative, so it has a negative acceleration.
- Uniform acceleration can also be calculated using the equation:

(final velocity)² – (initial velocity)² = 2 × acceleration × distance

$$v^2 - u^2 = 2as$$

Velocity–Time Graphs

- The **gradient** of a velocity–time graph can be used to find the acceleration of an object.

The total distance travelled is equal to the area under the graph.

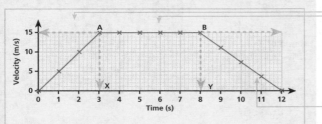

Distance travelled:

First section: $\frac{1}{2} \times 3 \times 15 = 22.5\text{m}$

Middle section: $15 \times 5 = 75\text{m}$

Final section: $\frac{1}{2} \times 4 \times 15 = 30\text{m}$

Total distance = 22.5 + 75 + 30

= 127.5m

Acceleration (a) is measured in metres per second squared (m/s²). Change in velocity (Δv) is found by subtracting initial velocity from final velocity ($v - u$) and is measured in metres per second (m/s). Time (t) is measured in seconds (s).

Final velocity (v) is measured in metres per second (m/s). Initial velocity (u) is measured in metres per second (m/s). Acceleration (a) is measured in metres per second squared (m/s²). Distance (s) is measured in metres (m).

The change in velocity is 15m/s over a 3 second period, so the acceleration is $\frac{15}{3} = 5\text{m/s}^2$

The velocity is constant, so the acceleration is zero.

The change in velocity is –15m/s over a 4 second period, so the acceleration is $\frac{-15}{4} = -3.75\text{m/s}^2$. The negative value shows that the object is slowing down.

Break down the area under the graph into smaller shapes.

Add together all of the areas to find the total distance.

Newton's Second Law

- Newton's second law is often stated as: the acceleration of an object is **proportional** to the resultant force acting on the object and **inversely proportional** to the mass of the object, i.e.
  - if the resultant force is doubled, the acceleration will be doubled
  - if the mass is doubled, the acceleration will be halved.
- This law can be summarised with the equation:

$$\text{force} = \text{mass} \times \text{acceleration}$$
$$F = ma$$

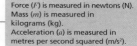

Force (F) is measured in newtons (N). Mass (m) is measured in kilograms (kg). Acceleration (a) is measured in metres per second squared (m/s²).

HT Mass is a measure of **inertia**.

HT It describes how difficult it is to change the velocity of an object.

HT This inertial mass is given by the ratio of force over acceleration, i.e. $m = \dfrac{F}{a}$.

HT The larger the mass, the bigger the force needed to change the velocity.

REQUIRED PRACTICAL	
Investigate the effect of varying the force and / or the mass on the acceleration of an object.	
Sample Method	**Considerations, Mistakes and Errors**
1. Set up the equipment as shown. 2. Release the trolley and use light gates or a stopwatch to take the measurements needed to calculate acceleration. 3. Move 100g (1N) from the trolley onto the mass holder. 4. Repeat steps 2 and 3 until all the masses have been moved from the trolley onto the mass holder. If investigating the mass, keep the force constant by removing a mass from the trolley but not adding it to the holder.	• When changing the force it is important to keep the mass of the system constant. Masses are taken from the trolley to the holder. No extra masses are added. • Fast events often result in timing errors. Repeating results and finding a mean can help reduce the effect of these errors. • If the accelerating force is too low or the mass too high, then frictional effects will cause the results to be inaccurate.
Variables • The independent variable is the force or the mass. • The control variable is kept the same. In this case, the force if the mass is changed or the mass if the force is changed.	**Hazards and Risks** • The biggest hazard in this experiment is masses falling onto the experimenter's feet. To minimise this risk, masses should be kept to the minimum needed for a good range of results.

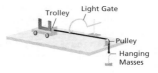

Trolley   Light Gate

Pulley

Hanging Masses

Quick Test

1. An object accelerates from 2m/s to 6m/s over a distance of 8m. **Use** the equation $v^2 - u^2 = 2as$ to find the acceleration of the object.
2. Comparing two velocity–time graphs, it can be seen that graph A is twice as steep as graph B. What does this indicate?
3. Why is it important to carry out repeat readings during an experiment?

> **Key Words**
>
> acceleration
> gradient
> proportional
> inversely proportional
> HT inertia

Terminal Velocity and Momentum

You must be able to:

- Draw and interpret diagrams showing how the forces on a falling object change as it approaches and reaches terminal velocity
- Give examples of Newton's third law in action
- HT Describe examples of conservation of momentum in collisions.

Terminal Velocity

- When an object falls through a fluid:
  - At first, the object accelerates due to the force of gravity.
  - As it speeds up, the resistive forces increase.
  - The resultant force reaches zero when the resistive forces balance the force of gravity. At this point the object will fall at a steady speed, called its terminal velocity.
- Near the Earth's surface, the acceleration due to gravity is 10m/s^2.
- The most common example of this is a skydiver:
  - ❶ The skydiver accelerates due to the force of gravity.
  - ❷ The skydiver experiences frictional force due to air resistance. Weight (W) is greater than the resistive forces (R), so the skydiver continues to accelerate.
  - ❸ Speed and R increase and acceleration decreases.
  - ❹ R increases until it is the same as W. At this point the resultant force is zero and the skydiver falls at terminal velocity.

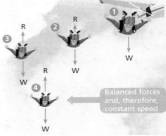

Balanced forces and, therefore, constant speed

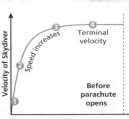

Newton's Third Law

- Newton's third law is often stated as: for every action there is an equal and opposite reaction.
- This means that whenever one object exerts a force on another, the other object exerts a force back.
- This reaction force is of the same type and is equal in size but opposite in direction.

HT Momentum

A rocket pushes fuel backwards, which in turn pushes the rocket forwards.

- All moving objects have momentum:

$$\text{momentum} = \text{mass} \times \text{velocity}$$
$$p = mv$$

Momentum (p) is measured in kilograms metres per second (kg m/s). Mass (m) is measured in kilograms (kg). Velocity (v) is measured in metres per second (m/s).

- When an unbalanced force acts on an object that is moving or able to move, a change in momentum occurs.
- Change in momentum can be calculated by substituting the equation for acceleration ($a = \frac{\Delta v}{t}$) into the equation for resultant force ($F = ma$):

$$F = \frac{m\Delta v}{\Delta t}$$

$m\Delta v$ is the change in momentum. Δt is the time over which the change takes place.

- This equation means: force equals rate of change of momentum.
- This is an important fact when considering many safety devices.
- These devices reduce the force by increasing the time over which the change of momentum takes place.
- For example, gymnasium crash mats cushion the impact of someone falling. They increase the time it takes for someone to come to rest when they fall onto the floor.

HT Conservation of Momentum

- In a closed system, the total momentum before an event is equal to the total momentum after the event.
- This conservation of momentum is most often referred to during collisions, but also applies to rockets and projectiles.

Two cars are travelling in the same direction along a road. Car A collides with the back of car B and they stick together.

Before

Car A mass 1200kg   Car B mass 1000kg

After

Car A + Car B mass 2200kg

Calculate the velocity of the cars after the collision.

Momentum before collision = momentum A + momentum B
= (mass A × velocity of A) + (mass B × velocity of B)
= (1200 × 20) + (1000 × 9)
= 24000 + 9000 = 33 000kg m/s

Momentum after collision = 33 000kg m/s
Momentum after collision = (mass A + mass B) × (new combined velocity)
33 000 = (1200 + 1000)v
33 000 = 2200v
$v = \dfrac{33\,000}{2200} = 15\text{m/s}$

HT Key Point

Momentum is the product of mass and velocity.

Force is the rate of change of momentum.

Conservation of Momentum

Recoil

Explosion

Rocket propulsion

Collision

Start by calculating the momentum before the collision.

Remember, momentum is conserved so: momentum before collision = momentum after collision.

Substitute in the values for momentum and mass.

Rearrange the equation to find the velocity.

Key Point

In a closed system, momentum is conserved.

Quick Test

1. HT Calculate the momentum of a 2000kg car travelling at 20m/s.
2. Use Newton's third law and the idea of equal and opposite forces to explain how a fish propels itself through water.
3. HT a) Calculate the momentum of a horse and rider with a total mass of 600kg travelling at 8m/s.
   b) A motorcycle and rider travelling at 12m/s has the same momentum as the horse and rider in part a). Work out the combined mass of the motorcycle and rider.

Key Words

terminal velocity
HT momentum
HT collision

Stopping and Braking

You must be able to:

- Interpret graphs that relate speed to stopping distance
- Describe factors affecting reaction time and braking distance
- Explain the dangers of large decelerations.

Stopping Distance

- The stopping distance of a vehicle depends on:
  - the thinking distance (the distance travelled during the driver's reaction time)
  - the braking distance (the distance travelled under the braking force).

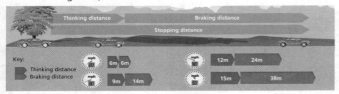

- For a given braking force: the greater the speed of the vehicle, the longer the stopping distance.

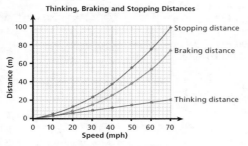

Thinking, Braking and Stopping Distances

- From the graph it can be seen that:
  - the thinking distance is directly proportional to speed
  - doubling the speed increases the braking distance by a factor of 4.

Reaction Time

- Reaction times vary from person to person, but the typical human reaction time is in the range of 0.2–0.9 seconds.
- This means that a car travelling at 30m/s (≈70mph) will travel between 12 and 27 metres before the person even begins to brake.
- This reaction time can be affected by tiredness, drugs and alcohol.
- Distractions, e.g. mobile phone use, also affect a person's ability to react.
- To measure reaction time, use lights or sounds as a 'start' signal and an electronic timer to measure how long someone takes to react.

Key Point

Stopping distance is the sum of the thinking distance and the braking distance.

Key Point

Reaction time can be affected by alcohol, drugs, fatigue and distractions.

- In the classroom, reaction times can be measured by dropping a ruler vertically and catching it as it falls.
- The distance the ruler falls through a person's fingers can be used to calculate the time it took them to react.

Factors Affecting Braking Distance

- The braking distance of a vehicle can be affected by the condition of the road, the vehicle and the weather.
- Adverse weather conditions include wet or icy / snowy roads.
- Vehicle condition includes factors such as worn brakes or tyres and over-inflated or under-inflated tyres.
- To stop a vehicle, the brakes need to apply a force to the wheels.
- The greater the braking force, the greater the deceleration of the vehicle.
- Work done by this frictional force transfers the kinetic energy of the vehicle into heat energy, increasing the temperature of the brakes.
- If the braking force is too large, the brakes may overheat or the tyres may lose traction on the road, resulting in the car skidding.
- Overheating and loss of traction are more likely to occur if the brakes or tyres are in poor condition.
- When a vehicle is travelling faster, it needs a larger braking force to be able to stop it in a certain distance.

HT To find the size of the braking force required, the equation for work done can be used:

> work done (kinetic energy) = force × distance (braking distance)

HT The table below shows the size of the braking force involved in two different braking situations:

Vehicle	Mass	Speed	Kinetic Energy	Braking Distance	Force
Car	1500kg	City ≈ 15m/s	168 750J	50m	3 375N
Lorry	7500kg	Motorway ≈ 30m/s	3 375 000J	50m	67 500N

The symbol ≈ means approximately equal to. Sometimes a single ~ is used to mean the same thing.

- For a given braking distance:
  - doubling the mass doubles the force required
  - doubling the speed quadruples the force required.

Quick Test

1. Explain what effect talking on a mobile phone might have on the stopping distance of a car.
2. HT Estimate the braking force needed to stop a 750kg motor cycle travelling at city speeds over a distance of 25m.
3. Describe a simple experiment to measure the reaction time of a person.

Key Words

braking distance
deceleration

Practice Questions

Forces – An Introduction

1 The mass of an object is a scalar quantity, but the weight of an object is a vector quantity.

Explain what is meant by this statement and the link between mass and weight. [4]

2 **Figure 1** represents the forces acting on an object.

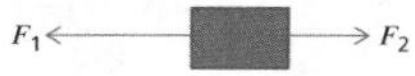

a) Compare the forces F_1 and F_2.

Figure 1

[2]

b) The force F_2 increases until it is of equal magnitude to F_1.

What will be the magnitude of the resultant force? [1]

3 **HT** **Figure 2** represents the resultant force acting on an object.

Draw the horizontal and vertical components of the arrow onto **Figure 2**.

Figure 2

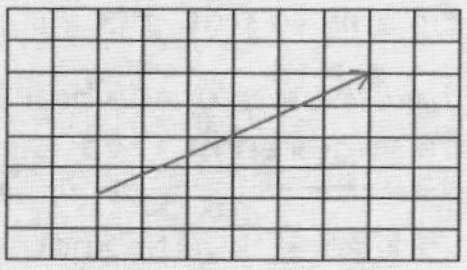

[1]

Total Marks _____ / 8

Forces in Action

1 A car travelling along a straight, level road at 30mph has 150kJ of kinetic energy.
The driver applies the brakes and comes to a complete stop in 50m.

a) What happens to the temperature of the brakes during braking? [1]

b) How much work is done by the brakes to stop the car? [1]

c) Calculate the braking force applied by the brakes. [2]

2 A wheelbarrow is loaded with 60kg of soil.
The load is a distance of 20cm from the wheel, which acts as the pivot point when the barrow is lifted.

a) Show that the soil weighs around 590N (g = 10N/kg). [2]

b) The handles of the wheelbarrow are positioned 60cm from the wheel.

Estimate the force needed to use the wheelbarrow to lift the soil. [2]

Total Marks _____ / 8

Pressure and Pressure Differences

1 Describe the cause of pressure in fluids. [2]

2 Write down the formula that links pressure, force and area. [1]

3 In a hydraulic system, the cross-sectional area of the left-hand piston is $\frac{1}{10}$ of the cross-sectional area of the right-hand piston.

If the left-hand piston is pushed down with a force of 100N, what force will be transferred to the right-hand piston? [2]

4 HT For this question you will need the following information:

> pressure =
>   height of the column × density of the liquid × gravitational field strength
> Gravitational field strength is 10N/kg.
> Density of water is 1000kg/m³.

a) A submarine descends from the surface to a depth of 100m.

Work out the increase in pressure. [3]

b) A swimming pool is 3m deep.

Calculate the pressure change experienced by swimmers when they swim from the bottom to the surface. [3]

5 A small boat floating on a lake experiences an upthrust 2597N.
(Use 10N/kg for the gravitational field strength.)

a) Calculate the mass of the boat to the nearest kilogram. [2]

The boat is loaded with an additional 100kg. It sits lower in the water but still floats.

b) What is the new total mass of the boat? [1]

c) Calculate the new value for the upthrust. [2]

d) Work out the volume of water displaced by the boat.
Density of water is 1000kg/m³.
$$\text{density} = \frac{\text{mass}}{\text{volume}}$$ [4]

Total Marks _____ / 20

Practice Questions

Forces and Motion

1 A hiker travels north for 2 miles, east for 1 mile and then south again for 2 miles.

    a) What is the total distance travelled?   [1]

    b) What is the final displacement?   [2]

2 The length of the race track at Silverstone is 3.65 miles.
A Formula One race is 52 laps of the race track.
The winner of the 2015 race completed the race in approximately 1 hour and 30 minutes.

    a) Calculate the following:

        i) The total distance travelled by one car during the race.   [1]

        ii) The displacement of the car at the end of the race, after completing 52 laps.   [1]

        iii) The average speed (in mph) of the winning car over the entire race.   [2]

    b) At some points in the race, the cars will be travelling at constant speed but their velocity will be changing.

       Explain how this can be true and where on the track this might occur.   [3]

3 **Figure 1** is a distance–time graph.

    a) How long is the object stationary for in total?   [1]

    b) During which part of the journey is the object travelling at the greatest speed.   [1]

    c) What is the speed between points **A** and **B**?   [2]

    d) If the graph contained curved lines, what would the curved sections indicate?   [1]

Figure 1

(distance–time graph: y-axis Distance (m) from 0 to 14; x-axis Time (seconds) from 0 to 14; points labelled A, B, C, D)

Total Marks _____ / 15

Forces and Acceleration

1 A car travelling at 10m/s accelerates at a constant rate of 4m/s² over a distance of 100m.

    Use the formula $v^2 - u^2 = 2as$ to work out the final velocity reached by the car.   [4]

2 **Table 1** shows the velocity of a remote-controlled car every two seconds for a 10 second period.

Time (s)	Velocity (m/s)
0	0
2	4
4	8
6	8
8	8
10	0

a) Plot a velocity–time graph for the 10 second period. [3]

b) Using your graph, describe the motion of the car between 5 seconds and 7 seconds. [1]

c) Calculate the acceleration of the car during the first 4 seconds. [2]

d) HT From your graph, calculate the total distance travelled. [3]

Total Marks _____ / 13

Terminal Velocity and Momentum

1 A falling object takes 0.4 seconds to accelerate from rest to a speed of 4m/s. Assuming that no other forces act on the object, show that the acceleration due to gravity is 10m/s². [3]

2 A helicopter weighs 25 000N.

a) What is the size of the upwards force that must act on the helicopter for it to remain hovering in a stationary position? [1]

b) Use Newton's third law to explain how the helicopter produces the force required in part a). [3]

Total Marks _____ / 7

Stopping and Braking

1 The airbags in a car inflate instantly in a crash and then deflate when a person hits them.

Explain how this helps to prevent injuries in terms of force, time and change in momentum. [4]

2 Give **three** factors that would have a negative effect on the reaction time of a driver. [3]

3 HT A lorry has a mass of 5000kg and is travelling at 12m/s. The driver applies the brakes and takes 5 seconds to come to a complete stop.

Calculate the braking force applied.

$$force = \frac{change\ in\ momentum}{time\ taken}$$

[2]

Total Marks _____ / 9

An Introduction to Electricity

You must be able to:

- Draw and interpret circuit diagrams
- Calculate the charge that flows in a circuit
- Relate current, resistance and potential difference
- Explain how to investigate factors that affect the resistance of an electrical component.

Standard Circuit Symbols

- In diagrams of electrical circuits:
  - standard circuit symbols are used to represent the components
  - wires should be drawn as straight lines using a ruler.
- You need to know all of the circuit symbols in the table below:

Component	Symbol	Component	Symbol
Switch (open)	—o o—	LED (light emitting diode)	
Switch (closed)	—o–o—	Bulb / lamp	
Cell		Fuse	
Battery		Voltmeter	—V—
Diode		Ammeter	—A—
Resistor		Thermistor	
Variable resistor		LDR (light dependent resistor)	

Electric Charge and Current

- Electric current is the flow of electrical charge – the greater the rate of flow, the higher the current.
- Current is measured in amperes (A), which is often abbreviated to amps, using an ammeter.
- Electric charge is measured in coulombs (C) and can be calculated with the equation:

LEARN

$$\text{charge flow} = \text{current} \times \text{time}$$
$$Q = It$$

> **Key Point**
>
> An ammeter is connected in series. A voltmeter is connected in parallel to the component.

Charge flow (Q) is measured in coulombs (C).
Current (I) is measured in amps (A).
Time (t) is measured in seconds (s).

- As the current in a single, closed loop of a circuit has nowhere else to go (i.e. no branches to travel down), the current is the same at all points in the loop.

Resistance and Potential Difference

- The resistance of a component is the measure of how it resists the flow of charge.
- The higher the resistance:
  - the more difficult it is for charge to flow
  - the lower the current.
- Resistance is measure in ohms (Ω).
- Potential difference (or voltage) tells us the difference in electrical potential from one point in a circuit to another.
- Potential difference can be thought of as electrical push.
- The bigger the potential difference across a component:
  - the greater the flow of charge through the component
  - the bigger the current.
- Potential difference is measured in volts (V) using a voltmeter.
- Potential difference, current and resistance are linked by the equation:

LEARN

$$potential\ difference = current \times resistance$$
$$V = IR$$

> ## Key Point
>
> Increasing the resistance reduces the current.
>
> Increasing the voltage increases the current.

> Potential difference (V) is measured in volts (V).
> Current (I) is measured in amps (A).
> Resistance (R) is measured in ohms (Ω).

REQUIRED PRACTICAL

Investigate the factors that affect the resistance of an electrical component.

Sample Method	Considerations, Mistakes and Errors
This example looks at how length affects the resistance of a wire: 1. Set up the standard test circuit as shown. 2. Pre-test the circuit and adjust the supply voltage to ensure that there is a measurable difference in readings taken at the lowest and highest temperatures. 3. Record the voltage and current at a range of lengths, using crocodile clips to grip the wire at different points. 4. Use the variable resistor to keep the current through the wire the same at each length. 5. Use the voltage and current measurements to calculate the resistance.	• Adjusting the supply voltage to ensure as wide a range of results as possible is important, as measurements could be limited by the precision of the measuring equipment. • The range of measurements to be tested should always include at least five measurements at reasonable intervals, e.g. 20, 30, 40, 50 and 60 degrees Celsius. This allows for patterns to be seen without missing what happens in between, but also without taking large numbers of unnecessary measurements.
Variables	**Hazards and Risks**

• The independent variable is the length of the wire.
 • The dependent variable is the voltage.
 • The control variable is the current (which is kept the same, because if it was too high it would cause the wire to get hot and change its resistance).
	• Current flowing through the wire can cause it to get very hot.
	 • To avoid being burned by the wire:
	   – a low supply voltage should be used, such as the cell in the diagram
	   – adjust the variable resistor to keep the current low.

Cell

Variable resistor

Ammeter (A)

Component

(V) Voltmeter

> ## Quick Test
>
> 1. A 600C charge flows in a circuit in 1 minute. What current is flowing?
> 2. Draw a standard test circuit for an investigation to measure the resistance of a diode.
> 3. A bulb has a 10V potential difference across it. A 2A current flows. What is the resistance of the bulb?

> ## Key Words
>
> current
> charge
> resistance
> potential difference
> precision

Circuits and Resistance

You must be able to:

- Interpret potential difference–current graphs
- Describe the shape of potential difference–current graphs for various components
- Use circuit diagrams to construct circuits.

Resistors and Other Components

- Potential difference–current graphs (V–I graphs) are used to show the relationship between the potential difference (voltage) and current for any component.
- A straight line through the origin indicates that the voltage and current are directly proportional, i.e. the resistance is constant.
- A steep gradient indicates low resistance, as a large current will flow for a small potential difference.
- A shallow gradient indicates a high resistance, as a large potential difference is needed to produce a small current.
- For some resistors the value of R is not constant but changes as the current changes, this results in a non linear graph.

> **Key Point**
>
> A V–I graph shows the relationship between voltage and current. It, therefore, can be used to determine the resistance.

REQUIRED PRACTICAL	
Investigate the V–I characteristics of a filament lamp, a diode and a resistor at constant temperature.	
Sample Method 1. Set up the standard test circuit as shown. 2. Use the variable resistor to adjust the potential difference across the test component. 3. Measure the voltage and current for a range of voltage values. 4. Repeat the experiment at least three times to be able to calculate a mean. 5. Repeat for the other components to be tested.	**Considerations, Mistakes and Errors** • Before taking measurements, check the voltage and current with the supply turned off. This will allow zero errors to be identified. • A common error is simply reading the supply voltage as the voltage across the component. At low component resistances, the wires will take a sizeable share of the voltage, resulting in a lower voltage across the component. This is why a voltmeter is used to measure the voltage across the component.
Variables • The independent variable is the potential difference across the component (set by the variable resistor). • The dependent variable is the current through the component, measured by the ammeter.	**Hazards and Risks** • The main risk is that the filament lamp will get hotter as the current increases and could cause burns. If it overheats, the bulb will 'blow' and must be allowed to cool down before attempting to unscrew and replace it.

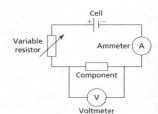

Cell

Variable resistor

Ammeter (A)

Component

Voltmeter (V)

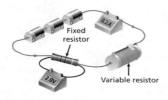

Fixed resistor

0.2A

2.0V

Variable resistor

Resistors

- An **ohmic conductor** is a resistor in which the current is directly proportional to the potential difference at a constant temperature.
- This means that the resistance remains constant as the current changes.
- It is indicated by a linear (straight line) graph.

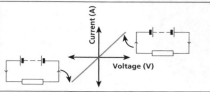

Filament Lamps

- As the current through a filament lamp increases, its temperature increases.
- This causes the resistance to increase as the current increases.
- It is indicated by a curved graph.

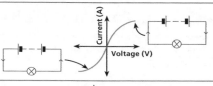

Diodes

- The current through a **diode** will only flow in one direction.
- The diode has a very high resistance in the reverse direction.
- This is indicated by a horizontal line along the x-axis, which shows that no current flows.

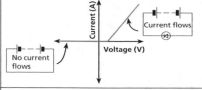

Thermistors

- The resistance of a thermistor decreases as the temperature increases.
- This makes them useful in circuits where temperature control or response is required.
- For example, a thermistor could be used in a circuit for a thermostat that turns a heater off at a particular temperature or an indicator light that turns on when a system is overheating.

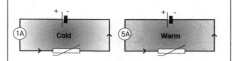

Light Dependent Resistors (LDRs)

- The resistance of an LDR decreases as light intensity increases.
- This makes them useful where automatic light control or detection is needed, e.g. in dusk till dawn garden lights / street lights and in cameras / phones to determine if a flash is needed.

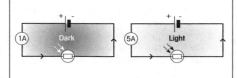

Quick Test

1. A V–I graph is plotted for a component. When the potential difference is negative, no current flows. What component has been tested?
2. A V–I graph is steep for high temperatures and shallow for low temperatures. What component does it represent?

Key Words

ohmic conductor
diode

Circuits and Power

You must be able to:

- Explain the difference between series and parallel circuits
- Explain the effect of adding resistors in series and parallel
- Explain what is meant by 'power', using examples
- Explain how the power transfer in any circuit device is related to the potential difference across it and the current through it, and to the energy changes over time.

Series and Parallel Circuits

- Electrical components can be connected in series or parallel.
- Some electrical circuits contain series and parallel parts.

Series Circuits	Parallel Circuits
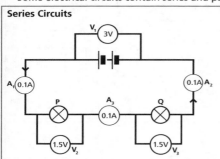	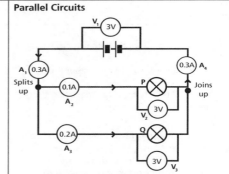
• There is the same current through each component.	• The potential difference across each component is the same.
• The total potential difference of the power supply is shared between the components.	• The total current drawn from the power supply is the sum of the currents through the separate components.
• The total resistance of two components is the sum of the resistance of each component. This is because the current has to travel through each component in turn.	• The total resistance of two resistors is less than the resistance of the smallest individual resistor. This is because, in parallel, there are more paths for the current to take – it can take one or the other, allowing it to flow more easily.
• Adding resistors in series increases the total resistance (R) in ohms (Ω): $R_{total} = R_1 + R_2$	• Adding resistors in parallel reduces the total resistance.

- You need to be able to calculate the currents, potential differences and resistances in d.c. parallel circuits.

A circuit containing two resistors in series has a 12V supply. R_1 is a 4Ω resistor and has a voltage of 8V across it.

a) Work out the voltage across R_2.

$V_{total} = V_1 + V_2$ ◄———— Remember, in a series circuit, the power supply voltage is shared.

$12 = 8 + V_2$ ◄———— Substitute in the given values.

$V_2 = 12 - 8 = 4V$ ◄———— Rearrange to find the voltage across the second resistor.

b) Calculate the current that flows in the circuit.

$V = IR$

$I = \frac{V}{R} = \frac{8}{4} = 2A$

The current flow is the same through every component, so it can be calculated using the known voltage and resistance of R_1.

c) Work out resistance of R_2.

$V = IR$

$R = \frac{V}{I} = \frac{4}{2} = 2\Omega$

Use the values for voltage and current calculated in parts **a)** and **b)**.

Key Point

You could also use equivalent resistance to answer part **c)**:

From the 12V supply, R_1 took 8V and R_2 took 4V. R_1 must be twice as difficult for current to flow through, i.e. it must have twice the resistance. Therefore, $R_2 = 2\Omega$

Power in Circuits

- The **power** of a device depends on the potential difference across it and the current flowing through it.
- A device with a higher potential difference or current will use more energy per second than one with a lower potential difference or current, i.e. it will be more powerful.

LEARN

power = potential difference × current

$P = VI$

power = (current)² × resistance

$P = I^2R$

Power (P) is measured in watts (W). Potential difference (V) is measured in volts (V). Current (I) is measured in amps (A). Resistance (R) is measured in ohms (Ω).

The heating element in a kettle produces an output power of 2300W when a potential difference of 230V is applied across it.

a) Calculate the current flowing across the element.

$P = VI$

$I = \frac{P}{V}$

$I = \frac{2300}{230} = 10A$

b) Work out the resistance of the element.

$P = I^2R$

$R = \frac{P}{I^2}$

$R = \frac{2300}{10^2} = \frac{2300}{100} = 23\Omega$

You could also use $V = IR$ here:

$R = \frac{V}{I} = \frac{2300}{10} = 23\Omega$

This is a useful way to double check your answers.

Quick Test

1. A series circuit with two resistors has a 6V supply. R_1 has a 5V potential difference across it. What can be said about the resistance of R_2 and what voltage will it have across it?
2. A torch bulb has a resistance of 6Ω. A current of 2A flows through it. Calculate the total power used by the bulb.
3. An oven has a 230V supply and a 30A current. Work out the power of the oven.

Key Words

series
parallel
power

Domestic Uses of Electricity

You must be able to:

- Explain the difference between direct and alternating current
- Describe a three-core cable
- Explain why a live wire may be dangerous even when a switch in the circuit is open
- Calculate the power of a device
- **HT** Understand how efficiency can be increased.

Direct and Alternating Current

- A **direct current (d.c.)** supply:
  - has a potential difference that is always positive or always negative – the current direction is constant
  - is the type of current that is supplied by cells and batteries.
- An **alternating current (a.c.)** supply:
  - has a potential difference that alternates from positive to negative – the current direction alternates
  - is the type of current used in mains electricity.

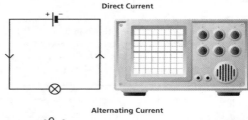

Direct Current

Mains Electricity

- Mains electricity in the UK is 230V and changes direction 50 times a second, i.e. it has a frequency of 50Hz.
- The mains supply uses three-core cable, i.e. the cable contains three wires.
- Each wire carries a different **electrical potential** and is colour-coded:
  - live wire (brown) – 230V potential
  - neutral wire (blue) – at or close to the 0V earth potential
  - earth wire (green and yellow stripes) – 0V potential.
- During operation:
  - the potential difference causes current to flow through the live and the neutral wires
  - the live wire carries the alternating potential from the supply
  - the neutral wire completes the circuit
  - current will only flow in the earth wire if there is a fault connecting it to a non-zero potential.
- The earth wire is a safety wire, which stops the exterior of an appliance becoming live.

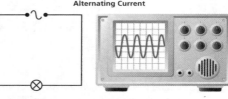

Alternating Current

The Three-Pin Plug

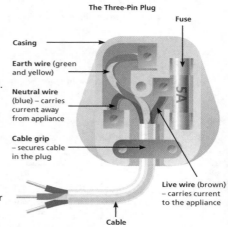

Fuse

Casing

Earth wire (green and yellow)

Neutral wire (blue) – carries current away from appliance

Cable grip – secures cable in the plug

Live wire (brown) – carries current to the appliance

Cable

Dangers of Mains Electricity

- Mains electricity can be very dangerous – an electric shock from a mains supply can easily be fatal.
- Touching the live wire can create a large potential difference across the body and result in a large current flowing through the body.

- The live wire can be dangerous even if a switch in the circuit is open.
- For example, a television might be switched off (so no current flows), but still plugged in and switched on at the wall:
  - The live wire between the wall and the switch on the television is still at an alternating potential.
  - All it needs is a path for the electricity to flow through.
  - This path could be provided by a damaged cable exposing the live wire.
  - If someone then touches the live wire, creating a potential difference from the live to the earth and causing current to flow, they will get an electric shock.

Power and Efficiency

- Power is the rate at which energy is transferred or work is done:

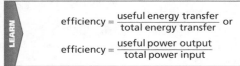

$$\text{power} = \frac{\text{energy transferred}}{\text{time}} \text{ or power} = \frac{\text{work done}}{\text{time}}$$

$$P = \frac{E}{t} \qquad\qquad P = \frac{W}{t}$$

- An energy transfer of 1J per second is equal to 1W of power.
- You must be able to demonstrate the meaning of power by comparing two things that use the same amount of energy but over different times.
- For example, if two kettles are used to bring the same amount of water to the boil and one takes less time, it is because it has a higher power.
- In an energy transfer, efficiency is the ratio of useful energy out to total energy in:
  - An efficiency of 0.5 or 50% means that half the energy is useful, but half is wasted.
  - An efficiency of 0.75 or 75% means that three-quarters of the energy is useful, but a quarter is wasted.

$$\text{efficiency} = \frac{\text{useful energy transfer}}{\text{total energy transfer}} \text{ or}$$

$$\text{efficiency} = \frac{\text{useful power output}}{\text{total power input}}$$

HT To increase the efficiency of an energy transfer, the amount of wasted energy needs to be reduced.

> **Key Point**
>
> Any connection between live and earth can be dangerous, because it creates a potential difference, causing a current to flow.

Power (P) is measured in watts (W).
Energy transferred (E) is measured in joules (J).
Work done (W) is measured in joules (J).
Time (t) is measured in seconds (s).

> **Key Point**
>
> Power is the rate at which energy is transferred.

> **Key Words**
>
> direct current (d.c.)
> alternating current (a.c.)
> electrical potential
> power
> efficiency

Quick Test

1. Describe the difference between alternating current and direct current.
   What is the voltage of the UK mains electricity supply?
   A 2.5V bulb has a current of 1.2A flowing through it. What is the power of the bulb and how much energy would it use in 10s?
   How much energy is transferred by a 2kW kettle in 50s?

Electrical Energy in Devices

You must be able to:

- Describe how different domestic appliances transfer energy
- Calculate the energy transferred by a device
- Describe the structure of the National Grid
- Explain why the National Grid is efficient.

Energy Transfers in Appliances

- Whenever a charge flows, it has to overcome the resistance of the circuit. This requires energy, therefore:
  - work is done when charge flows
  - the amount of work done depends on the amount of charge that flows and the potential difference.
- The amount of energy transferred can also be found from the power of the appliance and how long it is used for, e.g. a 20W bulb uses 20J of energy in every second.

LEARN

energy transferred = power × time

$$E = Pt$$

energy transferred = charge flow × potential difference

$$E = QV$$

Energy transferred (E) is measured in joules (J).
Power (P) is measured in watts (W).
Time (t) is measured in seconds (s).
Charge flow (Q) is measured in coulombs (C).
Potential difference (V) is measured in volts (V).

A 2kW heater is on for one hour. How much energy does it use?

1 hour = 60 minutes × 60 seconds = 3600 seconds

2kW = 2 × 1000W = 2000W

$E = Pt$

$\quad = 2000 \times 3600$

$\quad = 7\,200\,000$J

Start by converting the values into watts and seconds.

The given values are for power and time, so use the first equation.

Substitute in the values.

- Electrical appliances are designed to cause energy transfers.
- The type and amount of energy transferred between stores depends on the appliance.

Electrical
energy
2000J/s

Heat energy (for element) 160J/s (wasted)

Heat energy (to water) 1800J/s (useful)

Sound energy 40J/s (wasted)

 Key Point

The energy transferred by an appliance depends on the power and the time it is on for.

The National Grid

- The National Grid is a system of cables and transformers linking power stations to homes and businesses.

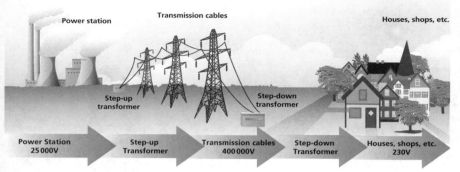

| Power Station 25 000V | Step-up Transformer | Transmission cables 400 000V | Step-down Transformer | Houses, shops, etc. 230V |

- Each component of the grid has a particular function.
- **Power station**:
    - The power station transfers the energy supply into electrical energy.
    - Using a smaller number of large power stations is more efficient than building many small, local power stations, because large stations can be made more efficient.
    - This is because most power plants use steam turbines, which are more efficient at higher steam temperatures, and the bigger the plant, the bigger the boiler, so the higher the steam temperature.
- **Step up transformers**:
    - The transformers increase the potential difference from the power station to the transmission cables.
    - This reduces the current and, therefore, reduces the heating effect caused by current flowing in the transmission cables.
    - Reducing the heating effect, reduces energy loss so makes the transmission more efficient.
- **Transmission cables**:
    - Transmission cables transfer the electricity.
- **Step down transformers**:
    - The transformers reduce the potential difference from the transmission cables to a much lower value for domestic use.

 Key Point

Electrical power is produced and transferred efficiently to consumers using the National Grid.

 Key Words

National Grid
transformer

Static Electricity

You must be able to:

- Describe how static electricity is produced by rubbing surfaces
- Describe evidence that charged objects exert a non-contact force
- Explain how the transfer of electrons between objects can produce static electricity
- Explain the concept of an electric field
- Draw the electric field pattern around a charged object.

Static Charge

- When insulating materials are rubbed against each other they can become electrically charged, e.g. when a balloon is rubbed against a jumper.
- The friction moves negatively charged electrons from one material to another:
  - The object that gains electrons becomes negatively charged.
  - The object that loses electrons becomes positively charged.
- Because the materials are insulators, the charge remains on the object.
- This effect would not be seen with conductors – they conduct the charge to earth so it cannot build up.
- An object that has no conducting path to earth is referred to as an isolated object.

The balloon is rubbed against the jumper

Paper then clings to the balloon

Electrical Sparks

- As the charge on an isolated object increases, the potential difference between the object and earth increases.
- When the potential difference becomes high enough, a spark may jump across the gap, from the object to any earthed conductor near to it.
- This spark discharges the charged object and could be felt as an electric shock.
- It could also serve as a source of ignition, which can be very dangerous, e.g. if the spark occurs in a petrol station.
- Lightning is an example of spark caused when a charge builds up in clouds during a thunderstorm.

Charge on a Van de Graaff generator can discharge with a spark as the charge flows to earth.

Electrostatic Forces

- Electrostatic forces are non-contact forces.
- They can be forces of attraction or repulsion.
- If a charged object is brought near an uncharged object, it can attract it.

Perspex Rod Repels a Perspex Rod

Perspex Rod Attracts an Ebonite Rod

Perspex Rod Rubbed with Cloth

Electrons

Ebonite Rod Rubbed with Fur

Electrons

- This can be seen when a charged plastic ruler is brought near to small pieces of paper or close to water running from a tap.
- When both objects carry the same charge, they will repel.
- When the objects carry opposite charges, they will attract.

Electric Fields

- A charged object creates an electric field around itself.
- The electric field can be thought of as the area around a charged object that will affect other objects, e.g. like a magnetic field.
- The strength of the electric field at any point depends on two factors:
  - the distance from the object – the further away from the object, the weaker the field
  - the amount of charge – the higher the charge, the stronger the field.

Tap

Charged plastic ruler

The density of electric field lines around these three objects reveals that the quantity of charge on **C** is greater than that on **B** which is greater than that on **A**.

- If a second charged object is placed in the field, it will experience a force.
- The force gets stronger as the objects get closer together.
- You need to be able to draw the electric field pattern for an isolated charged sphere.
- A field diagram can help to explain electrostatic forces:
  - Where the field lines are close together, the field is stronger, so the force exerted on another object is stronger and the greater the chance a spark will occur.
  - The direction of the arrow indicates the direction that a positive charge will move in if placed in the field and explains why like charges repel and unlike charges attract.

Field lines

The Electric Field from an Isolated Positive Charge

The Electric Field from an Isolated Negative Charge

Quick Test

1. A child sliding down a plastic slide builds up a charge. They receive a shock at the bottom when they touch the metal legs of the slide. Explain why this would not happen with a metal slide.
2. Two identical balloons are charged by rubbing them on the same jumper. They are then suspended side by side. Describe what will happen.
3. How will the field lines drawn around a small negative charge be different from those around a large positive charge?
4. An object is moved further away from a charged object. Use the idea of electric fields to explain how this will affect the force on the object.

Key Point

All charged particles produce an electric field around themselves.

Key Words

isolated
spark
attraction
repulsion

Review Questions

Forces – An Introduction

1 Complete the sentences.

There are two different types of force, contact and non-contact forces. .... ,

.... and electrostatic forces are examples of .... forces. Friction and

.... are .... forces that oppose motion. [5]

2 The gravitational field strength on the Moon is 1.6N/kg and the gravitational field strength of Earth is 10N/kg.

a) Calculate the weight of a 70kg astronaut on **i)** the Moon and **ii)** on Earth. [2]

b) Explain why an astronaut can jump higher on the Moon than on Earth. [2]

3 HT Use a vector diagram to show an object travelling with a driving force of 20N and a frictional force of 5N.

Your diagram should show:
- The driving force
- The frictional force
- The resultant force
- The size of the resultant force. [4]

4 HT An arrow in flight experiences air resistance of 0.5N and a gravitational force of 2N.

Show this on a scale vector diagram and add an arrow to indicate the resultant force. [3]

Total Marks .... / 16

Forces in Action

1 Write down the equation that shows the relationship between work done, force and distance. [1]

2 In a tall building, the height between floors is 3.5m.
The lift car that carries people between floors weighs 1200N.

Calculate the work done by the engines when the lift car is raised up five floors. [3]

3 Explain why at least two forces are needed to stretch a spring. [2]

4 A fisherman fixes a 4m fishing rod at the base creating a pivot.
He holds the rod 1m from the pivot.
A fish is caught and pulls away with a force of 12N.

Calculate the force the fisherman must apply to hold the rod still. [4]

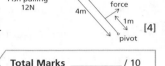

Fish pulling 12N

Fisherman force

4m

1m

pivot

> Total Marks _____ / 10

Pressure and Pressure Differences

1 In a hydraulic system, the cross-sectional area
of the left-hand piston is 0.1cm².
The area of the right-hand piston is 0.5cm².

If the left-hand piston is pushed down with a
force of 200N, what force will be transferred
to the right-hand piston? [2]

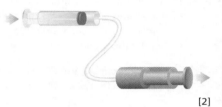

2 HT For this question, you will need to refer to the Physics Equations on pages 47-48.

Gravitational field strength is 10N/kg.
The density of mercury is 13 500kg/m³.

In a laboratory, a column of mercury is poured into a
measuring cylinder with a cross-sectional area of 3cm².

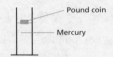

Pound coin

Mercury

a) Calculate the pressure at the bottom of a 10cm tall column of mercury. [3]

b) Calculate the weight of mercury that acts on the bottom of the measuring cylinder. [3]

c) When a pound coin is dropped into the mercury, it floats on the surface.

What conclusion can be drawn about the density of the pound coin? [1]

d) The pound coin has a weight of 0.1N.

Work out the weight of mercury that is displaced by the coin. [1]

3 At the top of a mountain the air pressure is lower than at sea level.

Explain why this is. [3]

> Total Marks _____ / 13

Review Questions

Forces and Motion

1. Describe the difference between speed and velocity. [2]

2. A hiker travels south for three miles, west for two miles and then north for one mile.

   a) What is the total distance travelled by the hiker? [1]

   b) HT Use a scale vector diagram to show the final displacement of the hiker? [2]

3. Sketch a distance–time graph to show the motion of an object that:
   • Accelerates gradually to a constant speed of 1m/s.
   • Remains at this speed for 2 seconds.
   • Decelerates gradually to come to rest having travelled 8 metres in total. [4]

4. HT Using an example, explain how an object can travel at constant speed but with a changing velocity. [3]

Total Marks _____ / 12

Forces and Acceleration

1. Write down whether each of the following statements is **true** or **false**.

   a) If the resultant force on an object is doubled, its acceleration will double. [1]

   b) If the force on an object is constant and the mass of the object increases, the acceleration will also increase. [1]

   c) Newton's second law states that for every force there is an equal and opposite reaction force. [1]

2. State what the following features would represent on a velocity–time graph.

   a) A straight line with a positive gradient. [1]

   b) A straight line with a negative gradient. [1]

   c) A horizontal line above the x-axis. [1]

   d) A horizontal line below the x-axis. [1]

   e) The area under the graph. [1]

Total Marks _____ / 8

Terminal Velocity and Momentum

1 Use Newton's third law and the idea of equal and opposite forces to explain why a hovercraft moves forward when the propeller spins. [3]

2 HT Write down the formula that links momentum, mass and velocity. [1]

3 HT A 240kg cannon fires a 1kg cannonball with a velocity of 120m/s.

Work out the velocity at which the cannon recoils backwards when it is fired. [4]

> Total Marks .... / 8

Stopping and Braking

1 Give **three** factors that would have a negative effect on the braking distance of a vehicle. [3]

2 HT Two students, Lisa and Jack, are discussing the braking of vehicles.
Jack thinks that if the braking force is the same but a car is going twice as fast, it will take twice the distance to stop.

Is he correct? You must explain your answer. [3]

3 Many long, downhill roads have an escape lane at the bottom for a driver to turn into if their brakes fail.

Explain why brakes are more likely to fail while travelling down a long, steep hill. [4]

4 A car travelling at 12m/s has a braking distance of 14m.

If the driver's reaction time is 0.5 seconds, what is the total stopping distance? [3]

> Total Marks .... / 13

Practice Questions

An Introduction to Electricity

1 Draw a diagram to show the circuit you would use to measure the voltage across a
bulb and the current through the bulb when connected to a battery. [4]

2 Name the component represented by each circuit symbol.

a) ⊣⊢ [1]   **c)** [1]

b) ─⊐⊏─ [1]   **d)** ─⊐⊐⊏─ [1]

3 A bulb is set up in a circuit.
When there is a potential difference of 12V across the bulb, a current of 0.5A flows.

a) Calculate the resistance of the bulb. [3]

b) The bulb is changed for a different type of bulb with half the resistance.

If the voltage remains unchanged, how will this affect the current that flows? [1]

Total Marks .... / 10

Circuits and Resistance

Figure 1

1 **Figure 1** shows the V–I graph for an ohmic conductor.

a) What can be deduced from **Figure 1** about the
resistance of an ohmic conductor? [1]

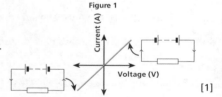

b) Add a second line to **Figure 1** to represent a different
ohmic conductor with a higher resistance than
the original. [2]

2 A circuit is constructed with a battery and LED.
The current through the LED is found to be 1.2A.

What would the current through the LED be if the battery was reversed? [1]

Total Marks .... / 4

Circuits and Power

1 **a)** Draw a series circuit with a 6V battery and three bulbs. [2]

b) Each bulb in your series circuit is identical.

Work out the potential difference across each bulb? [1]

c) The current through the battery is 2A.

Work out the current through each bulb. [1]

d) Use your answers to parts **a)** and **b)** to calculate the resistance of each bulb. [3]

e) What is the total resistance of the circuit? [1]

2 **a)** In a series circuit, what effect does adding additional resistors have on the total resistance of the circuit? [1]

b) In a parallel circuit, what effect does adding additional resistors in parallel have on the total resistance of the circuit? [1]

Total Marks .... / 10

Domestic Uses of Electricity

1 Name the **three** wires in a UK mains cable and, for each one, give its colour. [3]

2 Explain why touching a live wire will cause a large current to flow through the person touching it. [4]

You must refer to electrical potential and potential difference in your answer.

3 What is the function of a neutral wire in a circuit? [1]

4 In a plug, at what potential is the earth wire? [1]

Total Marks .... / 9

Practice Questions

Electrical Energy in Devices

1 Here is some information about a vacuum cleaner for sale in a shop:

Super Vac: 230V, 1000W Power, extra quiet, light weight, £120

   a) What is power a measure of? [1]

   b) Calculate the current supplied to the vacuum cleaner when it is working at maximum power. [3]

2 A circuit containing a 5kΩ resistor has a current of 0.1A running through it.

   a) Calculate the power being used by the resistor. [3]

   b) The circuit is switched on for two minutes.

      Calculate the energy transferred by the resistor in this time. [3]

3 Explain why the National Grid transfers electricity at a high voltage and low current. [2]

> Total Marks _____ / 12

Static Electricity

1 A balloon is rubbed on a jumper and becomes negatively charged.

   a) Explain in terms of particle movement how the balloon becomes negatively charged. [3]

   b) The balloon is moved close to some small pieces of ripped up paper.

      What would you expect to see happen? [1]

2 A Van de Graaff generator is used in a classroom to demonstrate static electricity.

   a) A student stands on an insulated tile with her hand touching
the top of the generator. Her hair stands up and sticks out.

      Explain why this occurs. [3]

   b) An earthed rod is brought close to the top of the generator.
A spark jumps across from the generator to the earthed rod.

      Explain why this occurs. [4]

> Total Marks _____ / 11

Review Questions

An Introduction to Electricity

1 A bulb has a current of 0.1A flowing through it.

   a) Calculate the amount of charge that is transferred if the bulb is turned on for 1 hour.   [3]

   b) The bulb is changed for a different type of bulb with twice the resistance.

      How would the voltage have to change for the same current to flow?   [1]

2 Circle the correct words to complete the sentences.   [4]

Resistance is a measure of how difficult it is for **voltage / current** to flow. Increasing the resistance means a bigger **voltage / current** is needed if the same **voltage / current** is to flow. A material with a very high resistance is called **a conductor / an insulator**.

3 A light emitting diode has a voltage of 2V across it and transfers 6C of charge per minute.

   a) Calculate the current that flows through the LED.   [1]

   b) Use your answer to part **a)** to calculate the resistance of the LED.   [1]

> **Total Marks** _____ / 10

Circuits and Resistance

1 The current–potential difference graphs for three electrical devices are shown in **Figure 1**.

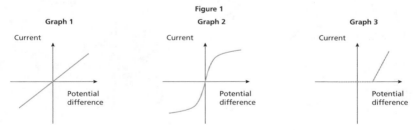

Figure 1

   a) Which graph corresponds to each of the components listed below?

     i) A diode.   [1]

     ii) A resistor at constant temperature.   [1]

     iii) A filament lamp.   [1]

Review Questions

b) Which graph shows a constant resistance? [1]

c) Which graph shows the resistance increasing as the current increases? [1]

Total Marks / 5

Circuits and Power

1. a) Draw a parallel circuit with a 2V battery and two bulbs. [3]

b) Each bulb in the circuit is identical.

Work out the potential difference across each bulb. [1]

c) The current through the battery is 2A.

Work out the current through each bulb. [1]

d) Use your answers to parts a) and b) to calculate the resistance of each bulb. [2]

Total Marks / 7

Domestic Uses of Electricity

1. Give the voltage and frequency of the UK mains electricity supply. [2]

2. **Figure 1** shows a three-pin plug.

Add the following labels to **Figure 1**.

Figure 1

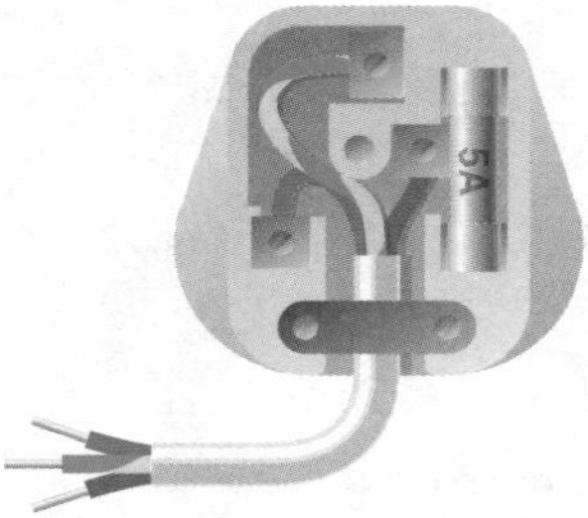

a) Earth Wire [1]

b) Live Wire [1]

c) Neutral Wire [1]

d) Fuse [1]

e) Cable Grip [1]

Total Marks / 7

Electrical Energy in Devices

1 Write down the formula that links power, potential difference and current. [1]

2 An electric heater has a power rating of 2.6kW and is connected to the UK mains supply (230V). The heater is used for 30 minutes.

   a) Calculate the current that flows in the heater. [3]

   b) Calculate the energy that has been transferred by the heater. [3]

   c) Calculate the charge that has been transferred by the heater. [3]

4 Using transformers in the National Grid means that energy can be transmitted from the power station to the user with very high efficiency.

   Give **three** reasons why this is important. [3]

Total Marks _____ / 13

Static Electricity

1 Static electricity can be produced when a charge builds up on an insulator or isolated object.

   a) What is meant by an 'isolated' object? [2]

   b) Why is it not possible to build up charge on a conductor that is not isolated? [1]

2 When a fuel tanker arrives at a petrol station, the driver always makes sure that the tanker is earthed before pumping fuel.

   Suggest why this is an important safety precaution. [3]

3 The arrows on an electric field line indicate the direction a positive charge will move in when placed within the field.

   On the diagrams in **Figure 2** add the field lines around the charged objects.

Figure 2

   The size of the charges is the same. [4]

Total Marks _____ / 10

Answers

Page 5 Quick Test
1. A scalar quantity just has size, but a vector has size and direction.
2. Magnetism / gravity / electrostatic attraction is a non-contact force; a magnet will attract or repel another magnet without needing to touch it / one mass will gravitationally attract another / one charge will attract or repel another charge without physical contact.
3. 128N   4. 100N to the east

Page 7 Quick Test
1. 100J   2. 37.5cm

Page 9 Quick Test
1. When particles collide with the surface of an object they exert a force. The pressure is the force per unit area.
2. 10000N 3. 900kg/m³ 4. 2000000Pa

Page 11 Quick Test
1. Distance is the total distance travelled in any direction; displacement is the total distance from the start point and includes the direction from the start point.
2. 20m/s   3. Speed

Page 13 Quick Test
1. 2m/s²
2. The object represented by graph A is accelerating at twice the rate of the object represented by graph B.
3. To identify anomalous results, which can then be removed and allow a mean to be taken.

Page 15 Quick Test
1. 40000kg m/s
2. As the fish swims it exerts a force backwards on the water. This creates an equal and opposite force from the water on the fish, that pushes the fish forwards.
3. a) $600 \times 8 = 4800$Nm
   b) $\frac{4800}{12} = 400$kg

Page 17 Quick Test
1. It might increase the stopping distance, as it increases the thinking distance by causing a distraction.
2. Answer should be between 2160N and 3375N using city speeds as 12–15m/s.
3. One person holds a ruler with the bottom of the ruler level with the other person's hand. They let go of the ruler and the other person catches it when they see it move. The reaction time is calculated from the distance the ruler falls before being caught.
   OR
   One person presses a switch that turns on a light and starts a timer. The other person presses a switch that stops the timer when they see the light.

Page 18 Forces – An Introduction
1. A scalar quantity has size only [1]; a vector quantity has size and direction

[1]; mass is the measure of how much matter is in an object [1]; weight is the force of gravity and, as a force, it acts in a particular direction [1]
2. a) F_1 is twice the size of F_2 [1]; and acts in the opposite direction [1]
   b) Zero   [1]
3. Correctly drawn vertical and horizontal arrows   [1]

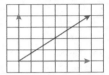

Page 18 Forces in Action
1. a) It increases   [1]
   b) 150000J   [1]
   c) $\frac{150000}{50}$ [1]; = 3000N [1]
2. a) 60×10 [1]; = 600N [1]
   b) Three times the distance of the soil from the pivot, so a third of the forced needed [1]; around 200N [1] (Accept accurate calculation of 196N)

Page 19 Pressure and Pressure Differences
1. It is caused by the random movement of the particles [1]; colliding with objects or the walls of a container [1]
2. pressure = $\frac{\text{force normal to a surface}}{\text{area of that surface}}$ / $p = \frac{F}{A}$ [1]
3. 10×100 [1]; = 1000N [1]

   Pressure is constant, so 10 times the area must be 10 times the force.

4. a) $100 \times 1000 \times 10$ [1]; = 1000000N/m² [2] (1 mark for correct value; 1 mark for correct units)
   b) The pressure falls by [1]; $3 \times 1000 \times 10$ [1]; = 30000N/m² [1]
5. a) $\frac{2597}{10}$ = 259.7 [1]; = 260kg (to the nearest kg) [1]
   b) 260 + 100 = 360kg   [1]
   c) 360×10 [1]; = 3600N [1]
   d) Mass displaced = 365kg [1]; volume = $\frac{\text{mass}}{\text{density}}$ [1]; = $\frac{365}{1000}$ [1]; = 0.365m³ [1]

Page 20 Forces and Motion
1. a) 5 miles   [1]
   b) 1 mile [1]; east [1]
2. a) i) 52×3.65 = 189.8 miles   [1]
      ii) 0 miles   [1]
      iii) $\frac{189.8}{1.5}$ [1]; = 126.5mph (to 1 decimal place) [1]
   b) This occurs when direction is changing [1]; but speed is constant [1]; so, could occur on bends / corners [1]
3. a) 3 seconds   [1]
   b) C to D   [1]

c) $\frac{3}{5}$ [1]; 0.6m/s [1]
d) Change in speed / acceleration and deceleration   [1]

Page 20 Forces and Acceleration
1. $v^2 = 2as + u^2$ [1]; $v^2 = (2 \times 4 \times 100) + 10^2$ [1]; $v^2 = 900$ [1]; $v = \sqrt{900}$ = 30m/s [1]
2. a) Correct axes and labels [1]; accurately plotted points [1]; straight lines joining points [1]

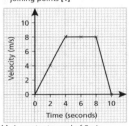

   b) A constant speed of 8m/s   [1]
   c) $\frac{8}{4}$ [1]; = 2m/s² [1]
   d) Area under graph divided into three sections [1];
   = $\frac{(8 \times 4)}{2} + (8 \times 4) + \frac{(8 \times 2)}{2}$ [1];
   = 56m [1]

Page 21 Terminal Velocity and Momentum
1. acceleration = $\frac{\text{change in velocity}}{\text{time}}$ / $a = \frac{\Delta v}{t}$ [1]; $a = \frac{(4 - 0)}{0.4}$ [1]; = 10m/s² [1]
2. a) 25000N   [1]
   b) The helicopter pushes the air downwards [1]; which creates an equal and opposite force from the air on the helicopter, which pushes the helicopter upwards [1]; when the force exerted on the air downwards is equal to the weight of the helicopter, the helicopter hovers at a constant height [1]

Page 21 Stopping and Braking
1. force = rate of change of momentum [1]; during a crash, the driver experiences a change of momentum and the faster this change happens, the bigger the force and the more serious the injury [1]; the airbag deflating increases the time that the change takes place over [1]; and, therefore, reduces the force on the driver [1]
2. Any three of: alcohol [1]; fatigue [1]; drugs [1]; distractions [1] (Accept specific distractions, e.g. mobile phone use)
3. $\frac{5000 \times 12}{5}$ [1]; = 12000N [1]

Page 23 Quick Test
1. 10A

2.

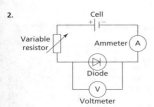

3. 5Ω

Page 25 Quick Test
1. Diode   2. Thermistor

Page 27 Quick Test
1. The resistance of R_2 is one-fifth that of R_1; it has a 1V potential difference across it
2. $P = I^2R = 2^2 \times 6 = 24W$
3. $P = IV$, $P = 30 \times 230 = 6900W$

Page 29 Quick Test
1. An alternating current changes direction rapidly and goes backwards and forwards; a direct current travels in one direction only.
2. 230V   3. 3W, 30J   4. 100 000J

Page 31 Quick Test
1. 2.5V
2. A Sankey diagram with an electrical input showing a 50/50 split between useful energy (heat and kinetic) and waste energy (heat and sound).

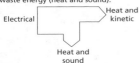

3. 3 600 000J
4. The power is generated in large stations; the electricity is transferred at high voltage / low current.

Page 33 Quick Test
1. A metal slide would earth the charge, so a charge could not build up.
2. They will repel each other.
3. The arrows around the large positive charge will point away from the charge and there will be many field lines. The small negative charge will have fewer field lines and the arrows will point inwards.
4. As it moves further away, the field lines are further apart so the field is weaker and the force is weaker.

Page 34 Forces – An Introduction
1. gravity [1]; magnetism [1]; non-contact [1]; drag [1]; contact [1] (Accept gravity / magnetism in any order)
2. a) i) $70 \times 1.6 = 112N$ **[1]**
      ii) $70 \times 10 = 700N$ **[1]**
   b) The force from the astronaut's legs, and the speed they would leave the

ground at, is unchanged **[1]**; but the force acting downwards is much less, so the astronaut travels higher before coming back down **[1]**
3. Correctly drawn driving force **[1]**; frictional force **[1]**; and resultant force **[1]**; resultant force of 15N stated **[1]**

Frictional 5N ←■→ Driving 20N
Resultant 15N

4. Correctly drawn air resistance **[1]**; gravitational force **[1]**; and resultant force **[1]**

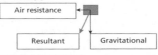

Page 34 Forces in Action
1. work done = force × distance (along the line of action of the force) / $W = Fs$ **[1]**
2. Five floors = $5 \times 3.5 = 17.5m$ **[1]**; work done = 1200×17.5 **[1]**; = 21 000J **[1]**
3. There needs to be two forces pulling in opposite directions **[1]**; or the spring would just move **[1]**
4. The fish exerts a moment of $12 \times 4 = 48Nm$ **[1]**; for the rod to remain still, the fisherman must exert an equal and opposite moment **[1]**; he must apply a force of $\frac{48}{1}$ **[1]**; = 48N **[1]**

Page 35 Pressure and Pressure Differences
1. Force = 200×5 **[1]**; = 1000N **[1]**

> The area is five times greater, so multiply by 5.

2. a) Height = 0.1m **[1]**; pressure = $0.1 \times 13500 \times 10$ **[1]**; = 13 500N/m² **[1]**
   b) force normal to a surface = pressure × area of that surface / $F = p \times A$ **[1]**; = 13500×0.0003 **[1]**; = 4.05kg **[1]**

> You need to use the equation $p = \frac{F}{A}$ and rearrange it to find the force. Don't forget to change the area from cm² to m² – 1cm² = 0.0001m².

   c) The pound coin is less dense than mercury **[1]**
   d) 0.1N **[1]**
3. There are few particles **[1]**; to collide with objects creating pressure **[1]**; and the height of air above is less **[1]**

Page 36 Forces and Motion
1. Velocity is a vector so has direction and magnitude **[1]**; speed has only magnitude **[1]**
2. a) $3 + 2 + 1 = 6$ miles **[1]**
   b) Correctly drawn vector diagram with three arrows showing the stages of the journey **[1]**; and one arrow showing the displacement **[1]**

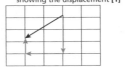

3. A sketch showing correctly labelled axes **[1]**; and a graph line with a gentle upward curve at the start **[1]**; followed by a straight, upward slope **[1]**; followed by a curved slope with a shallower gradient **[1]**

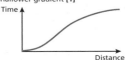

4. A planet in orbit / a roundabout / a car on a bend (any other sensible example) **[1]**; it is changing direction so the velocity changes **[1]**; but the magnitude of velocity i.e. the speed is constant **[1]**

Page 36 Forces and Acceleration
1. a) True **[1]**
   b) False **[1]**
   c) False **[1]**
2. a) Speeding up **[1]**
   b) Slowing down **[1]**
   c) Constant forwards / positive velocity **[1]**
   d) Constant backwards / negative velocity **[1]**
   e) Distance travelled **[1]**

Page 37 Terminal Velocity and Momentum
1. The blades on the propeller push the air backwards **[1]**; this creates an equal and opposite force of the air pushing on the hovercraft **[1]**; which moves it forwards **[1]**
2. momentum = mass × velocity / $p = mv$ **[1]**
3. Momentum of the cannon ball = $1 \times 120 = 120kgm/s$ **[1]**; since momentum is conserved, the momentum of the cannon is 120kgm/s in the opposite direction **[1]**;
   $= \frac{p}{240} = \frac{120}{240}$ **[1]**; = 0.5m/s **[1]**

Page 37 Stopping and Braking
1. **Any three of:** rain / snow **[1]**; old / worn tyres **[1]**; old / worn brakes **[1]**; poor road condition **[1]**
2. He is incorrect **[1]**; doubling the speed quadruples the kinetic energy **[1]**; so the brakes need to do four times the work and it takes four times the distance to stop **[1]**
3. Brakes use friction to slow the car **[1]**; this does work on the car by converting kinetic energy **[1]**; to heat energy **[1]**; on a long steep slope the brakes are more likely to overheat causing them to fail **[1]**
4. Thinking distance = $12 \times 0.5 = 6m$ **[1]**; braking distance = $6 + 14$ **[1]**; = 20m **[1]**

Page 38 An Introduction to Electricity
1. Diagram showing a correctly connected battery **[1]**; bulb **[1]**; ammeter **[1]**;

Answers

and voltmeter **[1]**

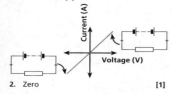

2. a) Cell **[1]**
   b) Variable resistor **[1]**
   c) LED **[1]**
   d) Thermistor **[1]**

3. a) resistance = $\dfrac{\text{potential difference}}{\text{current}}$ /

   $R = \dfrac{V}{I}$ **[1]**; = $\dfrac{12}{0.5}$ **[1]**; = 24Ω **[1]**

   b) Twice the current will flow **[1]**

Page 38 Circuits and Resistance
1. a) It is constant **[1]**
   b) A line drawn that passes through zero **[1]**; but is less steep than the first line **[1]**

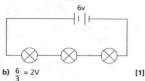

2. Zero **[1]**

Page 39 Circuits and Power
1. a) Diagram showing a correctly connected 6V battery **[1]**; and three bulbs in series **[1]**

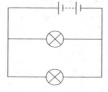

   b) $\dfrac{6}{3}$ = 2V **[1]**
   c) 2A **[1]**
   d) resistance = $\dfrac{\text{potential difference}}{\text{current}}$ /

   $R = \dfrac{V}{I}$ **[1]**; = $\dfrac{2}{2}$ **[1]**; = 1Ω **[1]**

   e) 3Ω **[1]**
2. a) Increases the total resistance **[1]**
   b) Decreases / reduces the total resistance **[1]**

Page 39 Domestic Uses of Electricity
1. Live – brown **[1]**; neutral – blue **[1]**; earth – yellow and green **[1]**
2. The live wire is at a high potential **[1]**; and a person is at zero **[1]**; touching the wire creates a large potential difference **[1]**; so a large current flows to earth through the person **[1]**

---

3. To complete the circuit **[1]**
4. 0V **[1]**

Page 40 Electrical Energy in Devices
1. a) The amount of energy transferred per second **[1]**
   b) power = potential difference × current / $P = VI$ **[1]**; $I = \dfrac{1000}{230}$ **[1]**; = 4.35A **[1]**
2. a) power = (current)² × resistance / $P = I^2R$ **[1]**; $P = 0.1^2 \times 5000$ **[1]**; 50W **[1]**
   b) energy transferred = power × time / $E = Pt$ **[1]**; $E = 50 \times 2 \times 60$ **[1]**; = 6000J **[1]**
3. It keeps the heating effect of the current low **[1]**; reducing wasted energy **[1]**

Page 40 Static Electricity
1. a) Electrons **[1]**; have been transferred from the jumper **[1]**; to the balloon **[1]**
   b) The paper would be attracted to the balloon **[1]**
2. a) All of the hairs become charged **[1]**; with the same type of charge **[1]**; so they are repelled from the head and each other **[1]**
   b) There is a large potential in the static charge on the generator **[1]**; and the rod is at earth **[1]**; so there is a large potential difference **[1]**; which, when large enough, causes a current to flow through the air as a spark **[1]**

Pages 41–43 Review Questions

Page 41 An Introduction to Electricity
1. a) 1 hour = 3600s **[1]**; $Q = 0.1 \times 3600$ **[1]**; = 360C **[1]**
   b) Twice the voltage would be needed **[1]**
2. current **[1]**; voltage **[1]**; current **[1]**; insulator **[1]**
3. a) 0.1A **[1]**
   b) 20 ohms **[1]**

Page 41 Circuits and Resistance
1. a) i) Graph 3 **[1]**
      ii) Graph 1 **[1]**
      iii) Graph 2 **[1]**
   b) Graph 1 **[1]**
   c) Graph 2 **[1]**

Page 42 Circuits and Power
1. a) Diagram showing correctly connected 2V battery **[1]**; and two bulbs in series **[2]** (1 mark for each correctly drawn pathway and bulb)

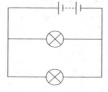

   b) 2V **[1]**

---

c) 1A **[1]**
d) resistance = $\dfrac{\text{potential difference}}{\text{current}}$ /

   $R = \dfrac{V}{I}$ **[1]**; = $\dfrac{2}{1}$ = 2Ω **[1]**

Page 42 Domestic Uses of Electricity
1. 230V **[1]**; 50Hz **[1]**
2. a) Correctly labelled earth wire **[1]**
   b) Correctly labelled live wire **[1]**
   c) Correctly labelled neutral wire **[1]**
   d) Correctly labelled fuse **[1]**
   e) Correctly labelled cable grip **[1]**

The Three-Pin Plug

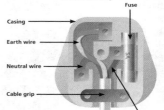

Page 43 Electrical Energy in Devices
1. power = potential difference × current / $P = VI$ **[1]**
2. a) current = $\dfrac{\text{power}}{\text{potential difference}}$

   / $I = \dfrac{P}{V}$ **[1]**; $I = \dfrac{2600}{230}$ **[1]**; = 11.3A **[1]**

   b) energy transferred = power × time / $E = Pt$ **[1]**; $E = 2600 \times 30 \times 60$ **[1]**; = 4 680 000J **[1]**
   c) charge flow = current × time / $Q = It$ **[1]**; $Q = 11.3 \times 30 \times 60$ **[1]**; = 20340C **[1]**
3. It saves resources **[1]**; reduces environmental damage **[1]**; saves money **[1]**

Page 43 Static Electricity
1. a) It is isolated from the earth **[1]**; by an insulator **[1]**
   b) It would conduct the charge to earth **[1]**
2. This makes sure there is no charge built up on the lorry **[1]**; which could make a spark **[1]**; and cause the fuel to ignite **[1]**
3. On first diagram: lines with arrows from positive to negative **[1]**; lines further apart as they get further away from centre **[1]**
   On second diagram: lines with arrows all pointing outwards **[1]**; lines further apart as they get further away from centre **[1]**

Physics Equations

You must be able to recall and apply the following equations using standard units:

Word Equation	Symbol Equation
weight = mass × gravitational field strength	$W = mg$
work done = force × distance (along the line of action of the force)	$W = Fs$
force applied to a spring = spring constant × extension	$F = ke$
moment of a force = force × distance (normal to direction of force)	$M = Fd$
pressure = $\dfrac{\text{force normal to a surface}}{\text{area of that surface}}$	$p = \dfrac{F}{A}$
distance travelled = speed × time	$s = vt$
acceleration = $\dfrac{\text{change in velocity}}{\text{time taken}}$	$a = \dfrac{\Delta v}{t}$
resultant force = mass × acceleration	$F = ma$
HT momentum = mass × velocity	$p = mv$
kinetic energy = 0.5 × mass × (speed)^2	$E_k = \frac{1}{2}mv^2$
gravitational potential energy = mass × gravitational field strength × height	$E_p = mgh$
power = $\dfrac{\text{energy transferred}}{\text{time}}$	$P = \dfrac{E}{t}$
power = $\dfrac{\text{work done}}{\text{time}}$	$P = \dfrac{W}{t}$
efficiency = $\dfrac{\text{useful output energy transfer}}{\text{useful input energy transfer}}$	
efficiency = $\dfrac{\text{useful power output}}{\text{total power output}}$	
wave speed = frequency × wavelength	$v = f\lambda$
charge flow = current × time	$Q = It$
potential difference = current × resistance	$V = IR$
power = potential difference × current	$P = VI$
power = (current)^2 × resistance	$P = I^2R$

Physics Equations

Word Equation	Symbol Equation
energy transferred = power × time	$E = Pt$
energy transferred = charge flow × potential difference	$E = QV$
density = $\dfrac{\text{mass}}{\text{volume}}$	$\rho = \dfrac{m}{V}$

The following equations will appear on the equations sheet that you are given in the exam. You must be able to select and apply the appropriate equation to answer a question correctly.

Word Equation	Symbol Equation
HT pressure due to a column of liquid = height of column × density of liquid × gravitational field strength	$p = h\rho g$
(final velocity)² – (initial velocity)² = 2 × acceleration × distance	$v^2 - u^2 = 2as$
HT force = $\dfrac{\text{change in momentum}}{\text{time taken}}$	$F = \dfrac{m\Delta v}{\Delta t}$
elastic potential energy = 0.5 × spring constant × (extension)²	$E_e = \frac{1}{2}ke^2$
change in thermal energy = mass × specific heat capacity × temperature change	$\Delta E = mc\Delta\theta$
magnification = $\dfrac{\text{image height}}{\text{object height}}$	
period = $\dfrac{1}{\text{frequency}}$	
HT force on a conductor (at right-angles to a magnetic field) = magnetic flux density × current × length	$F = BIl$
thermal energy for a change of state = mass × specific latent heat	$E = mL$
HT $\dfrac{\text{potential difference across primary coil}}{\text{potential difference across secondary coil}} = \dfrac{\text{number of turns in primary coil}}{\text{number of turns in secondary coil}}$	$\dfrac{V_p}{V_s} = \dfrac{n_p}{n_s}$
HT potential difference across primary coil × current in primary coil = potential difference across secondary coil × current in secondary coil	$V_s I_s = V_p I_p$
For gases: pressure × volume = constant	$pV = constant$